LEARN TO PLAY THE COUNTRY FIDDLE

Folk Violin (or fiddling) and Concert Violin do have a lot of things in common. Holding the Violin, fingerings, bowing, and good left hand position for rapid playing are common to both.

It is a quite common belief that no one can learn to play fiddle from a book, or reading music. Perhaps they are confused by the meaning of two words, playing and interpretation. I agree that interpretating a type of music cannot be learned from a book, it must come from within. The same can be applied to classical music. Interpretation or artistic performing can only be stimulated by a teacher. The same applies to country music.

If you do not have a fiddler friend who can play a tune over and over again or, if you cannot hum or whistle a tune until you remember it well enough to play it and learn it, note reading is the easiest way to learn.

Other details will be explained later in the book, as the student advances. This book is a very gradual course for quick and easy progress.

FRANK ZUCCO

1 2 3 4 5 6 7 8 9 0

Selecting A Violin

Select your Violin from a reputable firm. Seek the advice of an established teacher or player before making your selection. The bridge must be properly shaped for the correct height, at 1st and 4th string. A Full size fiddle must have a full size bow. Many stores have a rental plan which is helpful to students obtaining an instrument on a trial basis.

Tuning The Fiddle

There are several different ways of tuning a fiddle. It is best to start with standard tuning.

STANDARD TUNING

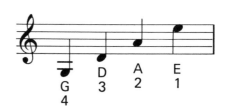

The four open strings of the fiddle will be the same pitch as the four notes shown in the illustration of the piano keyboard.

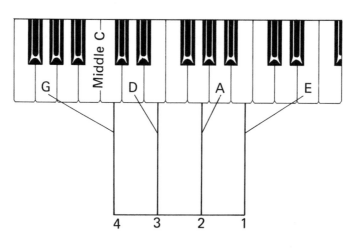

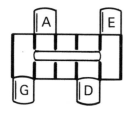

PITCH PIPES

Pitch pipes may be obtained at any music store, each pipe will have the exact pitch of the individual string of the fiddle.

They are recommended to be used when a piano is not available.

The Violin & Bow

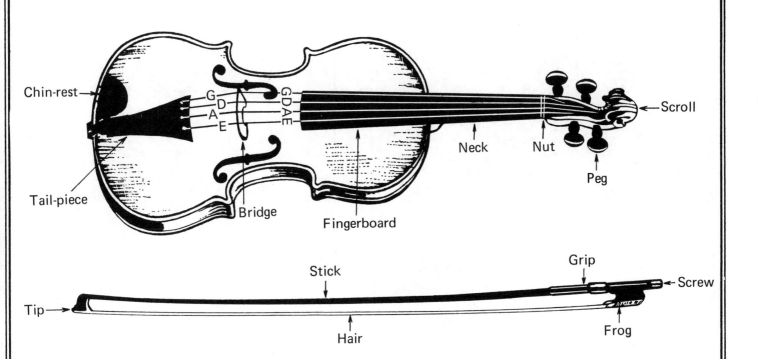

Chin-rest — Tail-piece — G D A E — G D A E — Bridge — Fingerboard — Neck — Nut — Peg — Scroll

Tip → Stick — Grip — Screw — Hair — Frog

(1) CHIN ON CHIN REST AND LEFT ARM

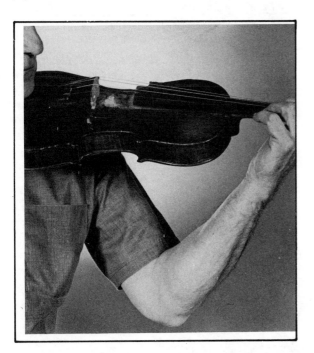

(2) LEFT HAND FINGERS (1 – 4)

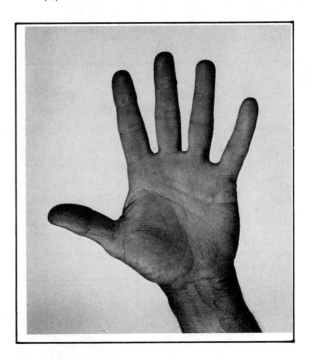

Holding the fiddle further down your chest, like some country fiddlers do, is not necessary. You can still play country fiddle holding fiddle like a Violinist, (under you chin resting on collar bone.) This position is better for a good tone, switching strings, and rapid playing.

More instructions and detail on hand, fingers, and bow follow.

Further Instructions On Holding The (Full Size) Fiddle

(1) Rest Position.

(4) Bend first finger and place tip on the "A" string (2nd string) about an inch from the nut. (Half size fiddle a little less.)

(2) Let the thumb rest on the neck, about one inch from the nut. Thumb almost straight.

(5) Without changing position of left hand, raise fiddle with right hand, place on collar bone. Chin on chin rest.

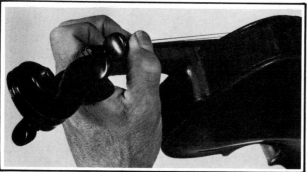

(3) Notice the Opening between the thumb and first finger. Never allow opening between thumb and first to close...must remain open at all times, even while playing.

(6) Left elbow well under fiddle. Place well curved fingers (finger tips only) down on string.

(7) Note well curved fingers.

Things To Remember

The fiddle can slant down slightly, keyboard in line with the eye. Hold the elbow well under fiddle. The nail of first finger should face you, when down on A and E strings. (1st and 2nd strings, slightly different on D and G or 3rd 4th strings.)

Holding The Bow

Bow is held in right hand, thumb slightly bent on frog. Curve fingers slightly over side of stick. Notice in the picture thumb and 3rd finger are separated by stick.

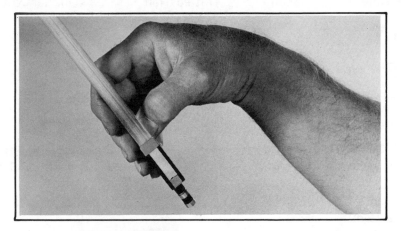

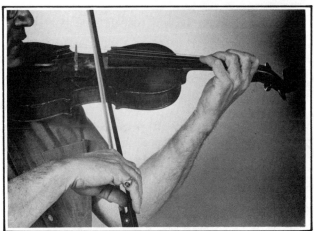

1   PICTURE OF BOW (MIDDLE)

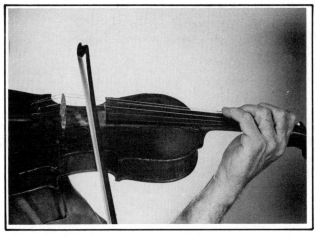

2   PICTURE OF BOW AT TOP

3   PICTURE OF BOW AT FROG

Figure (1) notice the bow, arm, wrist. Also notice the fingers of left hand.

Figure (2) -Bow remains between bridge and end of keyboard.

Figure (3) Notice the elbow down, and the wrist is bent slightly.

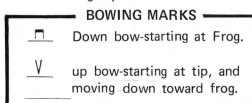

BOWING MARKS

⊓   Down bow-starting at Frog.

∨   up bow-starting at tip, and moving down toward frog.

Note Reading Versus Playing By Ear

Very few fiddlers read music. They either play by ear or they had someone, perhaps a relative or a good friend who drilled them frequently, teach them to play. Reading music is comparatively easy. There are only 7 notes(A B C D E F G)or (12) twelve in all, counting the sharps and flats. So, if you do not have a relative or a close friend who is a fiddler, reading notes is the answer.

THE TYPES OF NOTES

Whole Note	Half	Dotted Half	Quarter Note
𝅝	𝅗𝅥	𝅗𝅥.	♩

The type of note will indicate the length of its sound.

𝅝 This is a whole note. The head is hollow.

𝅗𝅥. This is a Dotted Half Note. The head is hollow. It has a stem and a dot.

𝅗𝅥 This is a half note. The head is hollow and has a stem.

♩ This is a quarter note. The head is filled in and has a stem.

𝅝 = 4 Beats. It will receive 4 beats or 4 counts

𝅗𝅥. = 3 Beats — a dotted half note receives 3 beats or 3 counts

𝅗𝅥 = 2 beats. It will receive 2 beats or 2 counts.

♩ = 1 beat. It will receive one beat or one count.

ABOUT COUNTING

Giving a note 4 beats or counts simply means sounding the note continually for 4 beats or counts. The same applies for 3 beats, 2 beats or one beat.

THE RESTS

Rests are signs of silence.

Space between two bar lines is called a measure.

Notes

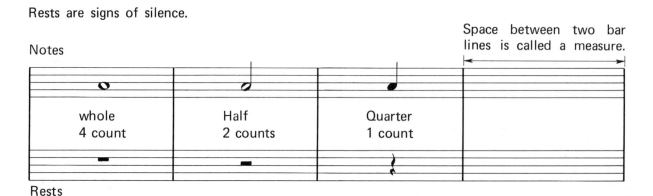

| whole 4 count | Half 2 counts | Quarter 1 count | |

Rests

The Time Signatures

4-The top number indicates the number of beats per measure.
4-The bottom number indicates the type of note receiving one beat.
4-Beats per measure.
4-A quarter note receives one beat.

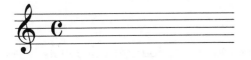

So called "common time" is simply another way of designating $\frac{4}{4}$ time.

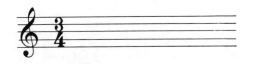

$\frac{3}{4}$ time = 3 beats per measure, each quarter note gets 1 full beat

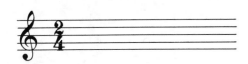

$\frac{2}{4}$ time = 2 beats per measure, each quarter note gets 1 full beat.

Bowing Exercise For Open Strings

To produce a clean tone, the bow should be held down on a straight line between the bridge and the end of the keyboard. Failing to bow properly will produce a very unpleasant, scratching sound.

Before proceeding, study Figures 1, 2 and 3 on Page 5.

Hold the right arm in a very relaxed manner. Bend the wrist slightly. Set the bow at the frog on the "A" string (2nd string). The fingers should be curved well above the string (but not touching other strings). Draw the bow very slowly towards the tip. Sound the "A" string as long as possible (this is down bow ⊓).

Stop bowing at the tip, and check the position of your hands. Left arm should be well under the violin. Now move the bow slowly up towards the frog. (This is up bow ∨).

Play a string as long as possible. Repeat this same exercise on all strings, stopping after each exercise to rest the left arm. Practice this open string exercise every day for several days until you gain good control of your Bow or Right Arm.

Signs And Abbreviations For Bowing

⊓ means down bow. ∨ means up bow. **W.B.** means Whole Bow. **M.H.** means middle half of bow.

TEMPO IS RATE OF SPEED

Ask yourself the question,"How fast should I count (1-2-3-4) when playing?"Well, just listen to the slow, steady tic of a Grandpa clock. For a starter, that will surely be fast enough.

The Notes On The Second String (A)

The Two Notes we will learn on The Second String are A (open) and B (first finger pressed down where shown on diagram)

The fingers must remain in line over the A string. Make sure they are well curved. Do not allow your little finger to drop. The picture shows the actual distance (whole step) between open A and B.

LET'S PLAY

Start at the frog (down bow ⊓). Draw the bow toward the tip slowly enough for four (4) full counts. Make a slight pause after each four (4) counts. Press the first finger down firmly to play B.

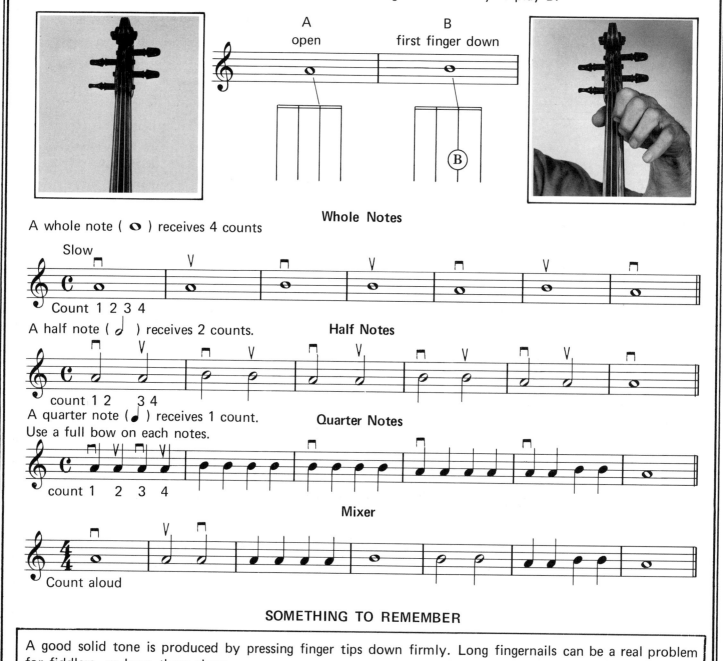

A whole note (o) receives 4 counts

A half note (d) receives 2 counts.

A quarter note (♩) receives 1 count.
Use a full bow on each notes.

SOMETHING TO REMEMBER

A good solid tone is produced by pressing finger tips down firmly. Long fingernails can be a real problem for fiddlers, so keep them short.

ANOTHER NOTE (Another Whole Step) — C♯ or "Raised C"

The picture shows the actual distance between all three notes as they are on the fiddle. I refer to C♯ as a "raised C". We do have a C (Low C) halfway between B and "raised C". For the present time, however, let us concentrate on C♯ or "raised C".

PITCH

Pitch is the highness or lowness of a musical sound. Try to sing the two whole steps we have learned.

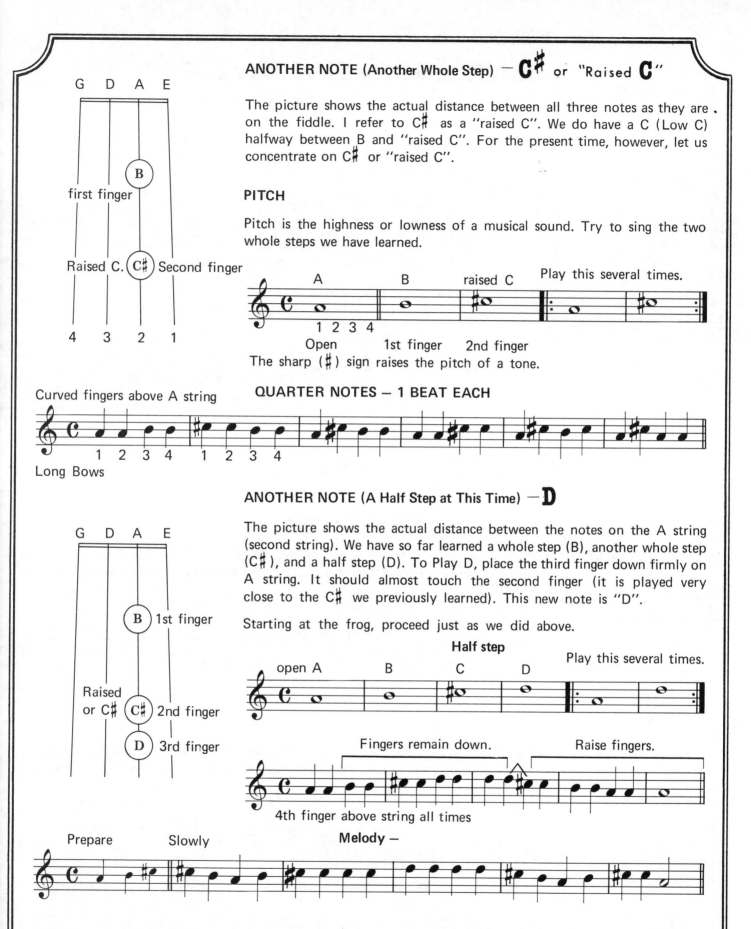

The sharp (♯) sign raises the pitch of a tone.

QUARTER NOTES — 1 BEAT EACH

ANOTHER NOTE (A Half Step at This Time) — D

The picture shows the actual distance between the notes on the A string (second string). We have so far learned a whole step (B), another whole step (C♯), and a half step (D). To Play D, place the third finger down firmly on A string. It should almost touch the second finger (it is played very close to the C♯ we previously learned). This new note is "D".

Starting at the frog, proceed just as we did above.

A half step is indicated by this sign (∧). A suggestion: Put the first finger down on B, and do not raise the first finger. Continue on in that manner. Raise the fingers only when you have to play the next note.

9

The Notes On The Third String (D)

G D A E

E 1st finger

F# 2 raised

G 3rd finger

The picture shows the actual distance of the whole step — whole step — half step. It is the same as on the "A" string, only the notes have changed. Keep the fingers well curved in line above the "D" string. Count slowly, bow slowly, and make a slight pause between the notes. When you have a half step (∧) hold the fingers close.

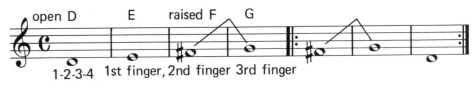

open D   E   raised F   G

1-2-3-4   1st finger, 2nd finger 3rd finger

Half Notes (𝅗𝅥) Two Beats Each
The letter names have been purposely omitted.

1-2 3 4

Warm up—Long Bow's

Mixer

1 2 3 4   1 2 3 4   1 2 3 4

Let's Try Two Strings

When moving from D string to A string, drop the right arm slightly. When going from A to D string, raise the right arm slightly. When changing strings, make a slight pause. The right arm must be free and relaxed at all times.

Slowly

Things To Remember

Before proceeding, study Figures 2 and 3 on Page 4. It is very important to maintain a proper hand position. When changing strings, the elbow should remain well underneath the fiddle. The hand never moves, only the fingers. Be sure to keep your wrist straight.

Long Bows

Mary

$\frac{4}{4}$ time is the same as "C". (Four beats to a measure, a quarter note gets one count.)

Something New — "Play Along"

Country fiddlers always have a guitar accompaniment. Get an early start at listening to the chords. Practicing the fiddle will be more fun and your sense of hearing will improve if you listen for the chords and especially, if you can practice with a guitarist.

A Change of Tempo — A Waltz
Review:

$\frac{3}{4}$ time equals three beats (or counts) to a measure. A quarter note gets one full beat or one count.
This is a dotted half note ($\dot{\downarrow}$). The half note receives two beats while the dot receives one beat. Therefore, a dotted half note receives three full counts.

Combinations of Different Rhythms

Count each variation aloud.

Sweet Betsy From Pike

Hand Position Long Bow's

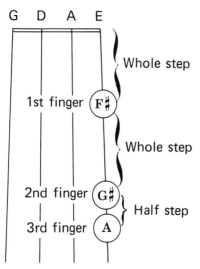

Time For A New String

The picture shows the exact distance between the fingers. You will notice that the distance is the same as the A and D strings. We now have two F sharps. A low F♯ is played with the second finger on the D string. A higher F♯ is played by placing the first finger on the E string where shown. We also may play a higher A than we previously learned by placing the third finger on the E string where shown.

Things to Remember

Before proceeding on the E string, carefully check the hand position. Page 4 – Figures 2, 3 and 4 are very important. The wrist must remain straight! Keep the fingers well curved above the string. Bow in the same manner as we did previously, starting at the frog and bending your wrist slightly. Move the bow towards the tip slowly enough for four full counts.

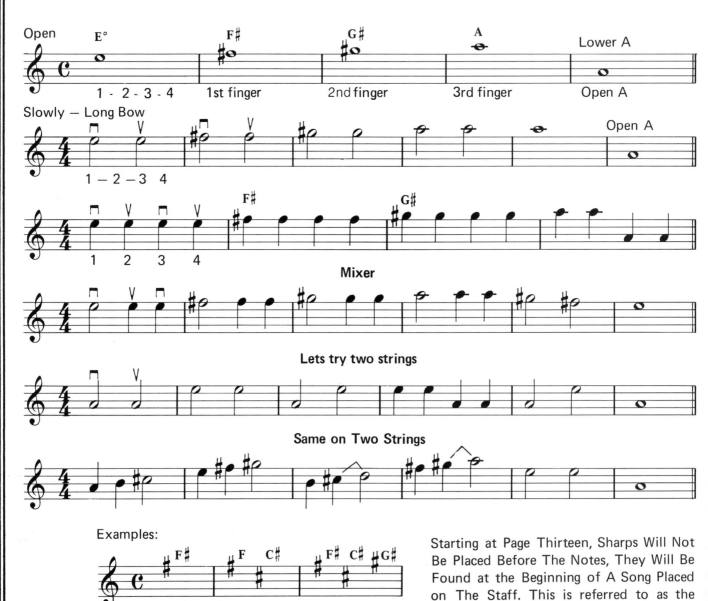

Starting at Page Thirteen, Sharps Will Not Be Placed Before The Notes, They Will Be Found at the Beginning of A Song Placed on The Staff. This is referred to as the **Key Signature.**

Tone Ladder With Guitar Chords (D Major Scale)

The sharp sign (♯) before the notes F sharp and C sharp has been purposely omitted.

Ain't You Something

F.C.Z.

Can be repeated again.

E & B Waltz

F.C.Z.

Warm up

Is your hand positioning good? Press your fingers down firmly. All fingers should be well curved over the strings. Keep your elbow well underneath the fiddle. Bow with good long even strokes. Good time and good rhythm mean good music. Count aloud. Listen carefully while you play the tune.

Read Carefully

Everyone who plays a musical instrument realizes that playing slowly is, no doubt, the best way to learn a tune. First, play slow, then later increase your tempo. The following tunes are to be played at a slow $\frac{4}{4}$ time. After playing them over several times, increase the tempos at your convenience. I am sure you will recognize the melodies. Here are a few examples:

Who's Dream?

A Cold Month

Fire Mountain

Etc.

The Notes On The Fourth String (G)

Time For a New String

The picture shows the actual distance between the whole step open G to A. Also, the whole step between A and B and the half step between B and C are shown. The fingers should be well curved. Keep your left elbow well under the fiddle to assure a good or solid arch. Keep your right arm slightly higher for the G string.

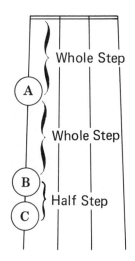

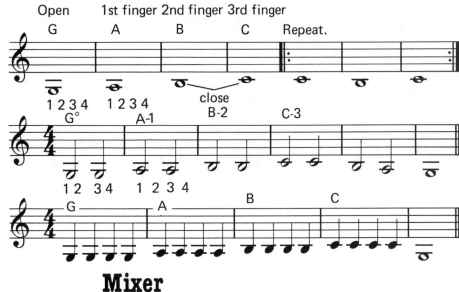

Letter names above notes have been purposey omitted.
— no sharps

Mixer

Check Point

This is a good time to review. Master the following exercises, especially the strings, notes, time and the positioning of the fingers on each string. We will not again review the subjects of the first seventeen pages. We must go on to new material.

Rests

(REVIEW FROM PAGE 6)

The Whole Rest
Whole rests hang down from the fourth line and they receive four full beats.

Half Rest
The Half Rest sits on the third line and it receives two beats.

The Quarter Rest
The quarter rest receives one full count.

Rests Are Signs Of Silence

Find The Mistake and Correct Each Measure.
Each measure must have four full beats.

Play Rest & Count Aloud.

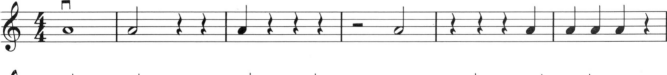

Three beats per measure.

1 2 3

16

The Eighth Note

The eight note receives one-half count. An eight note may look like this ♪ or several of them may look like this ♫. You may learn to count with the movement of your hand. A beat has two positions (the down beat and the up beat.) "D" will be the symbol for down and "U" will be the symbol for up. Place the left hand waist high and the right hand ten inches above the left hand. Begin a down-up, down-up, motion slowly and evenly. Count each movement aloud.

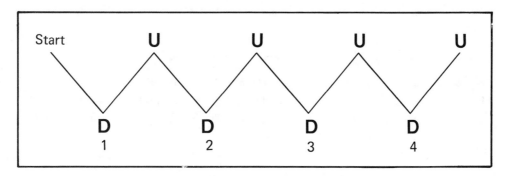

Proceed in the same manner. Substitute one and, two and, three and, four and, for down-up, down-up etc. for four beats.

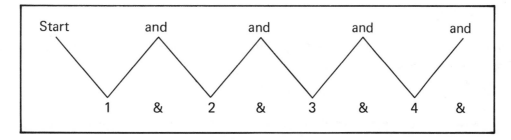

Combined Patterns for Eighth Notes

By playing a note on the down beat, and a note on the up beat, you are now playing two notes per beat.

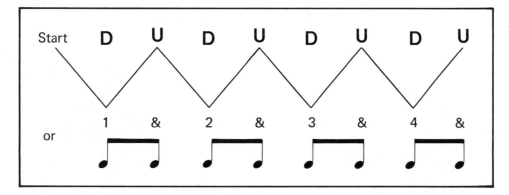

Things To Remember

Do not jerk your hand up or down. Maintain a slow steady pulse. Remember each 8th note must receive the same amount of time.

The Eighth Note Continued

Reviewing the down-up movement, here is another detail that could further your understanding of counting and playing. Study these examples carefully. Check Figure 1 on page 17 if necessary. The abbreviation for hand movements are: D for down, U for up, and (&) for "and". Count aloud and slowly.

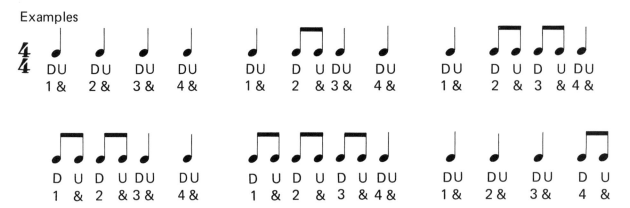

Examples

These are just a few patterns. Make up some of your own.

Play the above examples on all the open strings (G, D, A, E.) Count aloud. Give each quarter note its full value (one and.)

Important Things to Remember

Never rush or change the tempo when changing from one type of note to another. Maintain an even, steady beat. Here are a few examples.

Play the above examples on all the open strings.

A New Note (C♮)

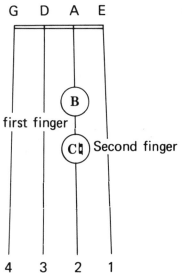

G D A E

first finger

B

C♮ Second finger

4 3 2 1

Warm up notes for Brother John

Brother John

Warm up for Aura Lee

Aura Lee

One Sharp In Key Signature

D string position and G string position are the same.

E string positions and A string are the same.

close

close

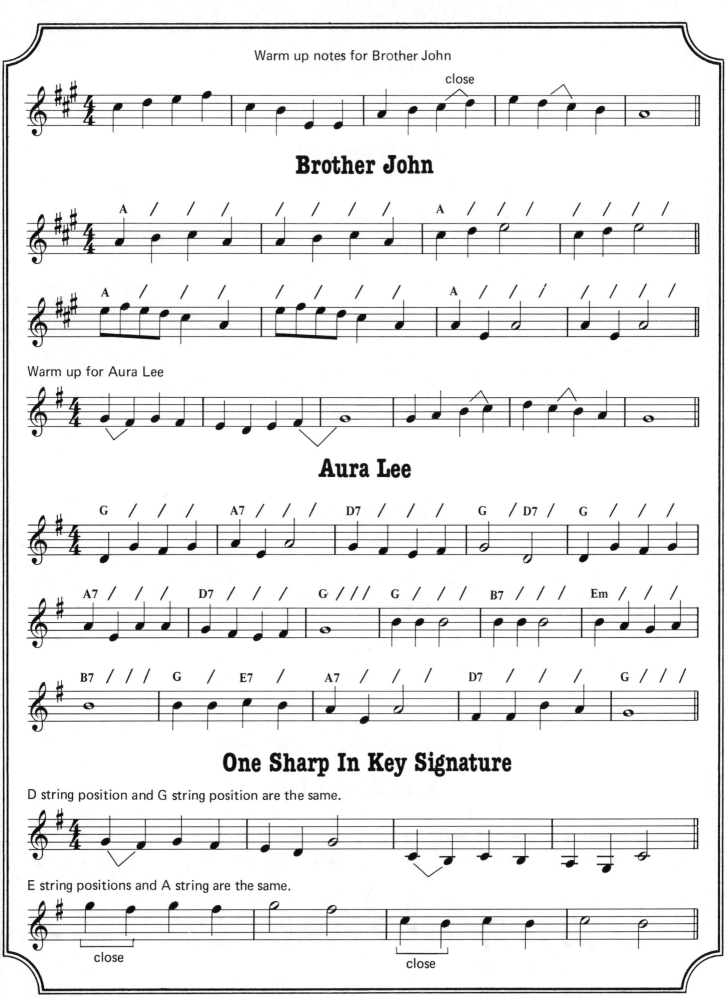

"Pick Up Notes"

The notes at the beginning of a song (before the first measure) are referred to as "pick up notes." The rhythm for pick up notes is taken from the last measure of the tune.

Red River Valley

Tone ladder — using the G and D string — G scale

Rhythm Scale

1 & 2 & 3 going up — coming down 1 — 2 — 3 & 4 &

Preparation for the next piece.
Practice on open strings.

Count 4 & 1 2 & 3 4 & 1 2 3 4 & 1 2 3 & 4 &

Ride Ranger Ride

Bowing Studies

Slurred Notes

A slur sign can be placed above the notes ♩♩♩ or, it may be placed below the notes ♩♩. This indicates that they are to be played in one bow. All of the notes must get equal division of the bow. Here are some examples. Remember, it is very important to count while you play.

One half of bow for each note.

One third of the bow for each note.

Four notes to one bow.

The slur sign applies only to different notes.

Tied Notes

The tie sign is the same in appearance as the slur sign. It also can be placed above or below the notes, but it has a different meaning. Tied notes are notes to be held over, not played again. Here are some examples. Count slowly and use long bows.

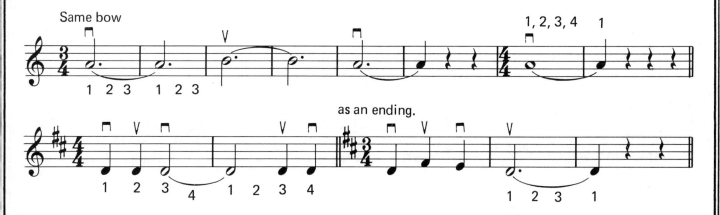

Things To Remember

Slurs and Ties are important in music. Never rush the tempo when playing a tied note. Remember, when playing ties or slurs, look ahead into planning your bowing.

The Natural (♮)

A natural sign placed before a note restores that note to its original pitch (it cancels out a sharp or a flat). When a natural sign cancels out a sharp, the pitch of that note is lowered to its original position. C♯ is lowered to C natural for example when a natural sign is placed before the C.

Sharps and natural signs are always placed before the note that is to be altered.

Repeat aloud

The flat Sign (♭)

Flats also can be placed before a note. A flat lowers the pitch of the note one half step.

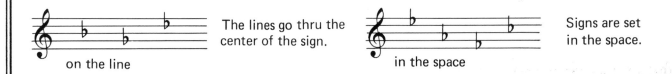

The lines go thru the center of the sign.

Signs are set in the space.

Flats are placed before the note that is to be altered.

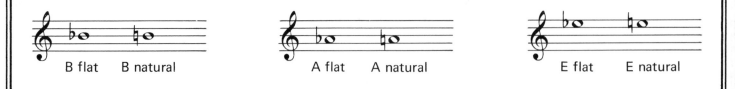

Writing the sharp, the flat, and the natural signs on all five lines and in four spaces will help you to determine what notes are affected by these signs.

Remember: The sharp raises the note, the flat lowers the note, the natural sign does either (it lowers a sharp to its original pitch and it raises a flat to its original pitch).

22

More About The Three Signs ♯–♮–♭

When reading music, learn to recognize the notes at a quick glance. This requires some practice. Learning to recognize where a sharp, flat, or natural is placed also requires some practice. The three signs will be placed at random on any line or space. The following examples are not to be played. Study them.

Starting with the lines

All on the third line.

The note the sharp, flat & natural sign

The Spaces

All in the space   Same applies for all spaces.

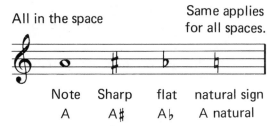

Note	Sharp	flat	natural sign
A	A♯	A♭	A natural

Write the three signs on the manuscript below using L for line, S — for space. See example.

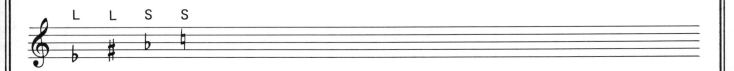

Include the letter name.

The Close – First & Second Finger Position

The half step between B and C (A string).

The first finger should remain down as a guide. Place your second finger down, almost touching your first finger.

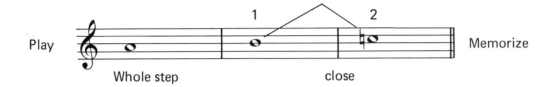

Play   Whole step   close   Memorize

Proceed on the D string in the same manner as above.

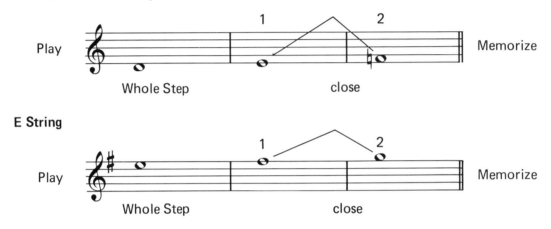

Play   Whole Step   close   Memorize

E String

Play   Whole Step   close   Memorize

To produce a half step requires us to play in "Close Position."

Things To Remember

The positions on the above strings are the same. Only the notes change. (Remember to hold your elbow well under the fiddle)

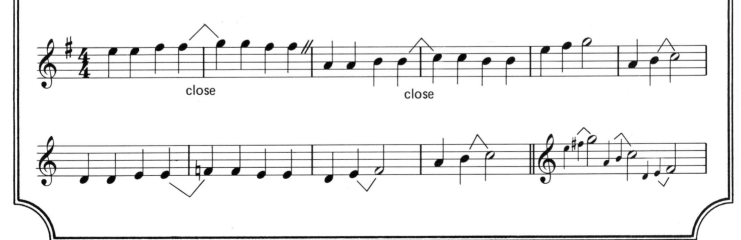

close   close

Open (A) String & First Finger (B♭)

This position is very close. The first finger must be strongly arched. Study the picture — number 2 on Page 4. For the thumb and hand position, hold the thumb and hand in the normal playing position. This never moves. Only the first finger should slide back and forth. The diagram shows the exact distance from B back to B♭.

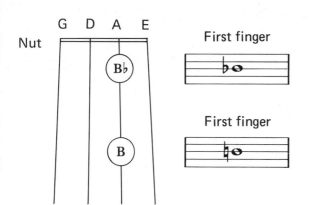

The distance between B flat to B natural is a half step. Study the diagram carefully before playing. Before proceeding check hand position.(Elbow well under fiddle, wrist straight, fingers well curved over A string.)Press first finger down firmly on B–Play for four counts–slight pause–slide first back to nut (B♭)–play for 4 counts–pause. Try to play in good tune.

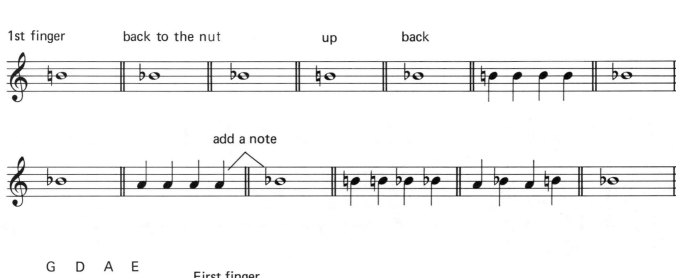

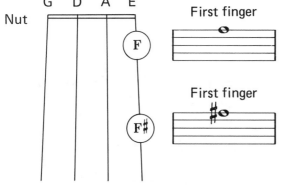

On the E string, F first finger to F♯ first finger, is the same as B♭ to B♮ on the A string. Proceed in the same manner. Remember, the positions are the same, only the notes change.

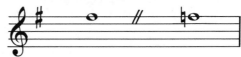

A New Key Signature F Major (B♭)

Tone Ladder with B♭

Prepare

At the nut   At the nut

0 1 2

Exercise for B♭

Exercise For (B♭)

Streets Of Laredo

Exercise For F

Prepare at the nut

0 F

E String Waltz

26

Write the alphabet letter above the note. The finger number and the string should be written below the note. Look at the example.

For Open String Write °A Or °D-°G-°E

An open circle means to play that string open.

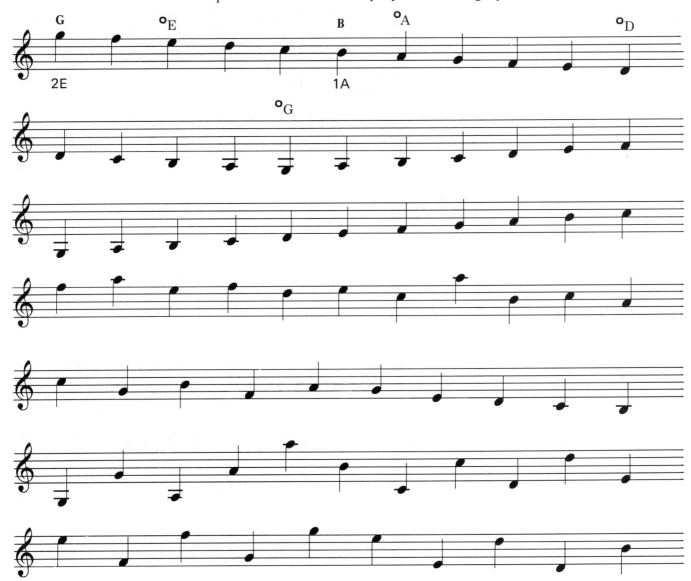

Review Of The Notes On The Fiddle

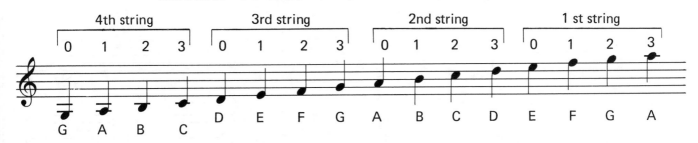

Master the above notes.

Preparation For The Key Of (C)

W.S. Whole step   Half step. = H.S. or ⌒
First finger remains down

Prepare

Anchor first finger —

close

Prepare   close

Old McDonald

Prepareo   0   1   2   3

Gee Bee

H.S.

Texas Waltz

H.S.   H.S.

28

Skip To My Lou

Count   1   2 & 3 & 4

I've Been Working On The Railroad

1   2   3 & 4 &

Hop-A-Long

Tone Ladder-C Major Scale

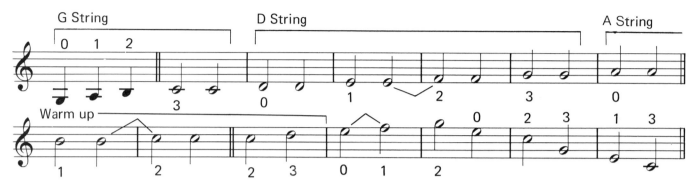

Red River Valley

Sing & Play Along Amazing Grace

Oh My Darling Clementine

Home On The Range

Country Dance Waltz On The G String

F.C.Z.

Buffalo Gals

Amazing Grace

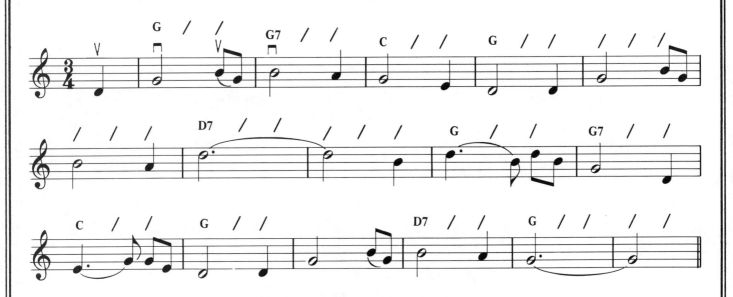

Sweet Hour Of Prayer

The Dotted Quarter Note

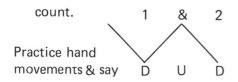 = 1 and ½beats

A dot after a note increases its value by one half count.

Practice hand movements & say

 Down up down or 1 & 2 } = 1 ½ beats

To complete two full counts add an eighth notes.

Written

Played

Preparation for next piece.

Count aloud

The Happy Farmer

Possible Rhythm Patterns

1 & 2 & 3 & 4&

1 & 2 &   3 & 4 &

1 & 2 & 3 & 4 &

The Repeat

Dots before and after a double bar mean repeat the measures between.

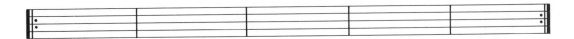

Good-Bye, Old Paint

Cowboy Jack

With a Little Variation

My Gal On The Rio Grande

The Fourth Finger

Of the four fingers, the fourth finger is the shortest. It is necessary to have a good position in order to play with the fourth finger.(Left elbow should be held well underneath the fiddle.)Curve your fingers well above each note. In the following studies, the first finger remains down as marked. Here are some examples.

Proceed In The Same Manner On The E String

D String

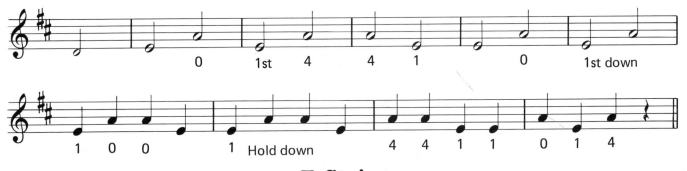

E String

37

Lightly Row

(USING THE FOURTH FINGER)

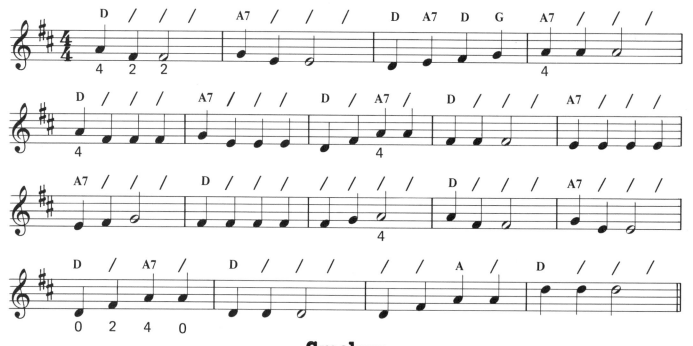

Smokey

Pretty Little Horses

Endurance Waltz

(a Tribute to Old Buck)

F.C.Z.

Double Stops

Playing more than one note simultaneously is referred to as a double stop. Playing thirds and octaves can be difficult to play in tune. Practice double stops slowly and carefully and listen carefully for the intonation.

Intervals

An interval is the distance or difference in pitch between any two musical sounds. Here are some examples.

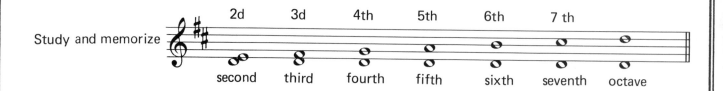

Intervals are recognized by the number of letters. From D to E is a second (2 letters). From D to F♯ is a third (3 letters D, E, F♯). D to G is a fourth (four letters D, E, F♯ G etc.). Practice the following slowly and listen to the different tones.

(Not too much pressure on the bow. Draw at an even pace. The two notes on the same stem are to be played together as a "double stop".)

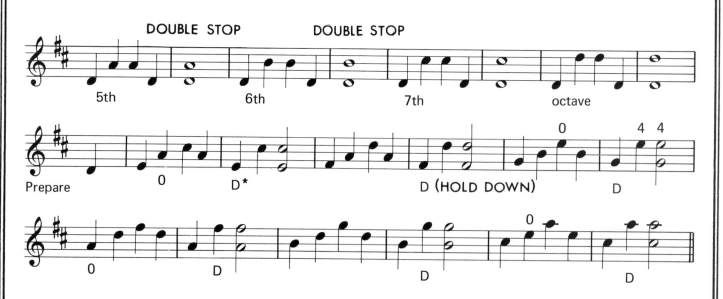

* When the letter D for down appears under a note, that note is to be held down as an anchor. Continue then on to the next note.

Double Stops Continued

Play carefully — D for Down

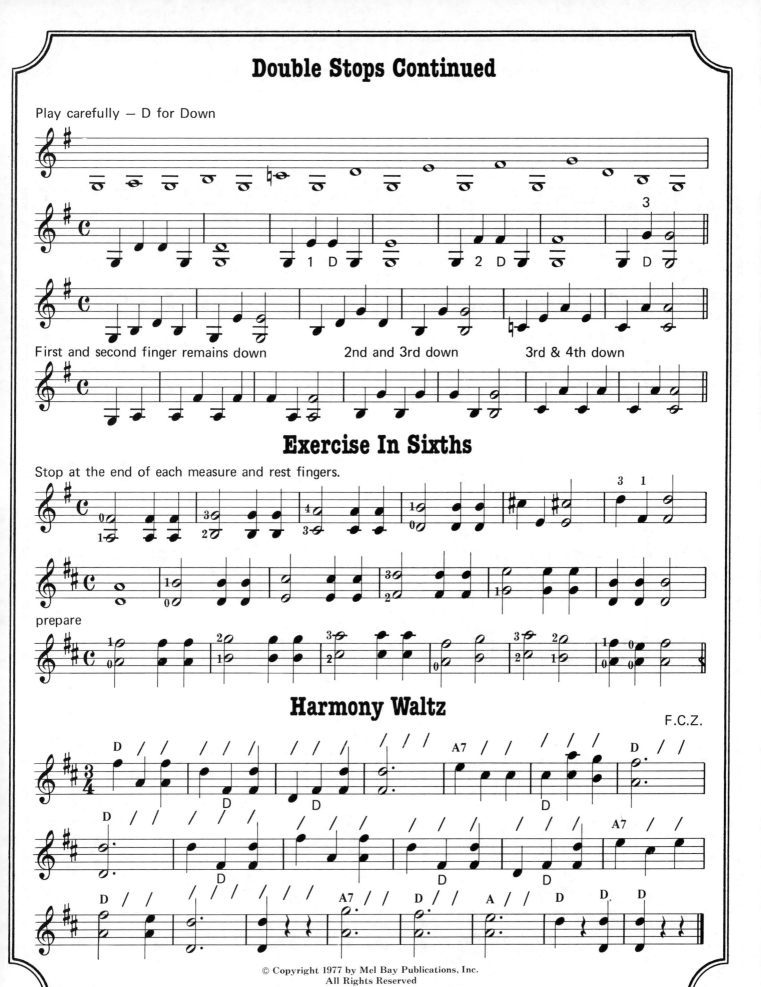

First and second finger remains down   2nd and 3rd down   3rd & 4th down

Exercise In Sixths

Stop at the end of each measure and rest fingers.

prepare

Harmony Waltz

F.C.Z.

The Colorado Lake George Waltz

Fiddlin' Matthew

F.C.Z.

Not too fast.

A Hymn Without Words

[Jesus, Forever]

Sweet By & By

44

O How I Love Jesus

Nothing But The Blood

Blessed Is The Name

Shall We Gather At The River

46

Liberty

Massa's In The Cold, Cold Ground

Foster

Nickie's Seven Up

F.C.Z.

Good Night Ladies